A JUST PASSION

A SIX-WEEK LENTEN JOURNEY

**RUTH HALEY BARTON,
SHEILA WISE ROWE,
TISH HARRISON WARREN,
TERRY M. WILDMAN, AND OTHERS**

An imprint of InterVarsity Press
Downers Grove, Illinois

InterVarsity Press
P.O. Box 1400 | Downers Grove, IL 60515-1426
ivpress.com | email@ivpress.com

InterVarsity Press® is the publishing division of InterVarsity Christian Fellowship/USA®. For more information, visit intervarsity.org.

Scripture quotations, unless otherwise noted, are from the New Revised Standard Version Bible, copyright © 1989 National Council of the Churches of Christ in the United States of America. Used by permission. All rights reserved worldwide.

Scripture quotations marked FNV are reproduced from *First Nations Version: An Indigenous Translation of the New Testament*, copyright © 2021 by Rain Ministries, Inc. Used by permission of InterVarsity Press. All rights reserved worldwide. www.ivpress.com

While any stories in this book are true, some names and identifying information may have been changed to protect the privacy of individuals.

The publisher cannot verify the accuracy or functionality of website URLs used in this book beyond the date of publication.

Cover design and image composite: David Fassett
Interior design: Daniel van Loon

ISBN 978-1-5140-0675-7 (print) | ISBN 978-1-5140-0676-4 (digital)

Printed in the United States of America ∞

Library of Congress Cataloging-in-Publication Data
A catalog record for this book is available from the Library of Congress.

8   7   6   5   4   3   2   1 | 29   28   27   26   25   24   23   22

CONTENTS

. . . .

*The Spirit of the Sovereign L*ORD *is on me,*
*because the L*ORD *has anointed me*
to proclaim good news to the poor.
He has sent me to bind up the brokenhearted,
to proclaim freedom for the captives
and release from darkness for the prisoners.

ISAIAH 61:1 NIV

. . . .

INTRODUCTION

L ent is a season of promise—we have ever before us the coming of Jesus' resurrection on Easter Sunday. Jesus is the one who in the glorious words of Isaiah will "proclaim good news to the poor," "bind up the brokenhearted," and "proclaim freedom for the captives" (Isaiah 61:1 NIV). But Lent is also a season of repentance. Isaiah continues in 61:8: "For I, the LORD, love justice; I hate robbery and wrongdoing."

Lent is an ideal time to explore what it means to love the justice of the Lord, and to consider whether there is any injustice in the way we live. For those who are in a place of privilege, Lent is a season for examining and confessing our complicity in injustice.

For those have experienced injustice in their own lives, Lent can be a part of a healing process as we follow Christ's journey through suffering and passion into resurrection. It is a season for lamenting the brokenness we have experienced in our lives and the world.

PRACTICING A JUST LENT

In her *Spiritual Disciplines Handbook*, Adele Calhoun defines justice as follows: "Justice seeks to help others through correcting and redressing wrongs. It treats others fairly and shows no favoritism." She says that justice has at its root the desire "to love others by seeking their good." She offers the following practices that we might consider as we seek to live out a call to justice:

- being responsible to God and others
- being a good steward of what you own
- supporting just causes with time, action, and financial support
- treating others impartially and fairly
- providing for the poor, needy, and oppressed through the means available to you
- volunteering for prison ministry, food-bank work, and ministries that serve needs in the local community
- refusing to buy products of companies that take advantage of the poor

Alongside your Lenten reading, consider which of these practices—either giving something up or taking up a new practice—will support you in the desire to focus on both God and neighbor.

THE SHAPE OF THIS BOOK

Tianna Haas, assistant project editor at IVP, has pulled and organized these readings from InterVarsity Press books. The author and book title are noted at the start of each reading.

We have intentionally left Sundays open with no readings as Sunday is a day of sabbath rest. In the liturgical tradition during Lent, sabbath is a day of feasting during which Lenten disciplines of fasting are set aside. Feel free to use this day to catch up on your reading if desired.

Each week you will also find two other repeated features. The first is a lectionary reading from the *First Nations Version*

(FNV). The FNV is a New Testament in English by Native North Americans for Native North Americans and all English-speaking peoples.

The other feature is a breath prayer that is designed to give you space to rest. In breath prayer, we breathe in praying a short line of invitation or supplication to God and then breathe out praying a line of response or release. Breath prayer helps us to calm our minds and recenter our thoughts on God. A variation of the Jesus Prayer from the Eastern Orthodox tradition can be prayed as a breath prayer and is an ideal prayer for the season of Lent.

Breathe in: Lord Jesus Christ, Son of God.

Breathe out: Have mercy on me, a sinner.

In his book *Lent*, Esau McCaulley offers readers this invitation: "We should not see the season of Lent as a series of rules, but as a gift of the collected wisdom of the church universal. It is one of many tools of discipleship pointing us toward a closer walk with Jesus." In the same spirit this devotional is designed to be a companion for you in the Lenten season, but not a burden or a source of guilt. Use it in the way that best fits your spiritual journey.

Cindy Bunch, IVP vice president, editorial, and author of *Be Kind to Yourself*

HOLD ON TO WHAT'S REAL

TISH HARRISON WARREN, *PRAYER IN THE NIGHT*

All go to one place; all are from the dust,
and all turn to dust again.

ECCLESIASTES 3:20

Each year, I need the reality of death proclaimed over me and over my children. I need my church community to remind me of my mortality. I can be tempted to skip too quickly to the resurrection, to skim over the sad stuff, but the liturgical calendar requires me to pause and notice the unresolved chord of our present reality.

At my very first Ash Wednesday service, over a decade ago, I knelt in a quiet sanctuary and was surprised by a feeling of almost irrepressible rage. As the priest marked each forehead with a cross of ashes, I felt like he was marking us for death. I was angry at death. I was angry at the priest as if it was somehow his doing.

I don't want to face the reality of vulnerability—especially the vulnerability of those I love. I'm privileged and healthy enough to maintain the illusion of control. I distract myself from the howling fury of suffering and mortality. I check

Facebook. I tweet. I immerse myself in the current political controversy. I get busy. I fill up my life with a thousand other things to avoid noticing the shadow of death.

But I can't shake it. I bump up against it in big and small ways each day. Sleep, sickness, weariness, and nighttime itself are ordinary and unbidden ashes on our foreheads. They say to us: remember that you are going to die. And these daily tokens of mortality are then transformed, by God's mercy, into tools for good works.

When I became a priest, I was suddenly the one marking others with a memento of their death each Lent. In some ways, I love serving as a priest on Ash Wednesday. It is utterly countercultural. Into our shiny, privileged American optimism the ancient church speaks. She forces us to face hard facts. Amid the temptation to a trite denial of mortality, I stand before the church with an unavoidable truth: "Don't forget," I say, "we are dust. You and I and everyone we know will die. The stuff we live for is fleeting. Hold on to what's real."

Tish Harrison Warren is a weekly contributing newsletter writer for the *New York Times* and writes a monthly column for *Christianity Today*. She is a writer-in-residence at Resurrection South Austin, a priest in the Anglican Church in North America, and a senior fellow with The Trinity Forum.

AGENCY FOR CHANGE

ESAU McCAULLEY, *READING WHILE BLACK*

The Spirit of the Lord is upon me,
because he has anointed me
to bring good news to the poor.
He has sent me to proclaim release to the captives
and recovery of sight to the blind,
to let the oppressed go free,
to proclaim the year of the Lord's favor.

LUKE 4:18-19

This theme of God's value of the undervalued, highlighted by Jesus, runs right through the New Testament. Paul speaks about it when he says, "God chose what is low and despised in the world, things that are not, to reduce to nothing things that are" (1 Corinthians 1:28). (It is important to note that these people are not actually lowly or despised by God, but rather society doesn't value them.) James argues much the same in his letter when he says, "Listen, my beloved brothers and sisters. Has not God chosen the poor in the world to be rich in faith and to be heirs of the kingdom that he has promised to those who love him?" (James 2:5).

It is important to point out that the "gospel" preached here and elsewhere does more than affirm the value of the poor.

Jesus seems them as moral agents capable of repentance. Stated differently, it is often stated that "good news" for the poor is bread or a job or political freedom. That is true insofar as it goes. But Jesus also cared about the *spiritual lives* of the poor. He saw them as bodies and souls. His call to repent acknowledges the fact that their poverty doesn't remove their agency. The poor are capable of sin and repentance. Repentance means that even if they remain poor, they can do so as different people. The enslaved recognized this. We see this on page after page of their testimony. Yes, they longed for actual freedom (no excessive spiritualization here) but they also rejoiced in the change wrought in their lives by the advent of God.

Jesus' ministry and the kingdom that he embodies involves nothing less than the creation of a new world in which the marginalized are healed spiritually, economically, and psychologically. The wealthy, inasmuch as they participate in and adopt the values of a society that dehumanizes people, find themselves opposing the reign of God. This dehumanization can take two forms. First, it can treat the poor as mere bodies that need food and not the transforming love of God. Second, it can view them as souls whose experience of the here and now should not trouble us. This is false religion that has little to do with Jesus.

Esau McCaulley is associate professor of New Testament at Wheaton College and a contributing opinion writer for the *New York Times*. He is also the author of *Sharing in the Son's Inheritance* and the children's book *Josey Johnson's Hair and the Holy Spirit*.

PRAYER AND HEALING

SHEILA WISE ROWE, *YOUNG, GIFTED, AND BLACK*

Do not be anxious about anything, but in every situation, by prayer and petition, with thanksgiving, present your requests to God. And the peace of God, which transcends all understanding, will guard your hearts and your minds in Christ Jesus.

PHILIPPIANS 4:6-7 NIV

The journey of healing from experiences of injustice is an intensely emotional process that cannot be rushed or ignored. It doesn't occur in an orderly way with fixed steps. No two people will heal precisely the same. Increasingly, we become aware of the emotional baggage from the past, and we seek to offload it so we can freely move forward. Famed Nigerian novelist Chinua Achebe wrote in "The Art of Fiction No. 139" for *The Paris Review*, "If you don't like someone's story, write your own." I believe this is a call to uncover and recover from the words and wounds written on our hearts, minds, and bodies by someone else.

Prayer is a two-way communication where we have the assurance that God hears us and wants to answer the most resounding cries of our hearts. As we learn to listen for God's voice and distinguish it from other voices, know that God always speaks to us from a place of love and with compassion and mercy. Even when asking us to face difficult truths about ourselves or a situation, God's messages always lead to clarity, release, and relief. If you hear a message that is mean-spirited or demoralizing, it isn't God speaking.

Although Jesus states, "I am the good shepherd; I know my sheep and my sheep know me. . . . They too will listen to my voice, and there shall be one flock and one shepherd. . . . My sheep listen to my voice" (John 10:14-16, 27 NIV), some of us question if we can hear from God. The Lord is constantly speaking to us, and he is willing and able to communicate in many ways. The Holy Spirit will bring us into all truth, whether it's through the Word, a still small voice, prayer, a situation, a person, pictures, or a gut-level hunch. Our part is to make the time and place to get quiet enough to pray and listen and remain open to his voice as we go about our day.

Jesus always welcomes us. He is the firm foundation where we can stand secure.

Sheila Wise Rowe holds a master's degree in counseling psychology and has ministered to abuse and trauma survivors in the United States and Johannesburg, South Africa. She is the cofounder of The Cyrene Movement and a writer, counselor, speaker, and spiritual director in the Boston area.

SABBATH ECONOMY

RUTH HALEY BARTON, *EMBRACING RHYTHMS OF WORK AND REST*

Six days you shall labor and do all your work. But the seventh day is a sabbath to the LORD your God; you shall not do any work—you, or your son or daughter, or your male or female slave, or your ox or your donkey, or any of your livestock.

DEUTERONOMY 5:13-14

One day a week we practice trusting in God as our ultimate strength and provider rather than putting all our faith in what we can secure for ourselves through our 24-7 striving. We practice humility and dependence on God as we settle into the limits of our humanity and rest one day a week. Remembering how we used to live and how God has freed us from our bondage leads quite naturally to delight and devotion as we determine once again that we will not get sucked back into a life of non-freedom. Sabbath is first and foremost about the freedom to live our lives on God's terms for us rather than living in bondage to anyone, anything, or any culture. It is about the God who is free to cease laboring and to rest, marking out a path for us to live in freedom as well.

And sabbath is not just for the privileged few. The passage from Deuteronomy reflects the fact that in its original context, sabbath was intended to be the great equalizer, ensuring that all God's creatures—including the animals!—would receive the benefits of this life-enhancing pattern.

One concern we might have about sabbath-keeping is that it smacks of privilege, an impossibility for those living in poverty, working multiple jobs, or perhaps "hustling" low-paying jobs to make ends meet. It is important to realize that this is an issue created by our current culture, not one created by the practice itself as God gave it.

Norman Wirzba, a professor at Duke Divinity school who pursues research and teaching at the intersections of theology, philosophy, ecology, agrarian, and environmental studies, goes even farther. In *Living the Sabbath* he articulates the idea of a *sabbath economy* in the spirit of our God who executes justice for the oppressed, gives food to the hungry, sets prisoners free, and lifts up the bowed down (Psalm 146:7-9). Wirzba defines a sabbath economy as one that will have "the *equitable distribution of resources* as a foremost goal."

We might not know exactly how to bring about this kind of equality in our current culture, but that does not change the fact that in God's economy sabbath is the great equalizer—the great leveler—and it is our job to figure out how to make it so today. A faithful sabbath practice actually calls us to it.

 **Ruth Haley Barton** is founder of the Transforming Center, a ministry dedicated to strengthening the souls of pastors and Christian leaders, and the congregations and organizations they serve. Her books include *Strengthening the Soul of Your Leadership*, *Pursuing God's Will Together*, and *Invitation to Retreat*.

FAILURE AND FORGIVENESS

DOMINIQUE DuBOIS GILLIARD,
RETHINKING INCARCERATION

Help us, O God of our salvation,
for the glory of your name;
deliver us, and forgive our sins,
for your name's sake.

PSALM 79:9

Biblically, justice is a divine act of reparation where breached relationships are renewed and victims, offenders, and communities are restored. Justice, therefore, is about relationships and our conduct within them. Justice asks, How is righteousness embodied and exuded in how I live in relation to God, neighbor, and creation? In fact, Scripture could be read as the narrative of God's restorative justice unfolding in the world.

Biblical justice is established and worked out within the confines of relationship. The relational working out of justice is righteousness. This is why Scripture calls us to pursue right(eous) relationships with God, neighbor, and creation, and through our realigned relationship with God, in Christ, empowered by the Holy Spirit, we "become the righteousness of God" (2 Corinthians 5:21 NIV).

While most people think about God's holiness, private morality, or spiritual prudence when they see the word *righteousness*, scripturally *righteousness* is most commonly used to define those who conduct themselves uprightly in all of their relationships. A righteous person treats all people—whether rich, poor, or condemned—with justice, generosity, and equity (Timothy Keller, *Generous Justice*). The two ancient words translated as "righteousness" in Scripture, *tsedeq* (Hebrew) and *dikaiosynē* (Greek), are used to define someone who has "lived uprightly and behaved justly before God and their neighbor" (Theopedia).

The liturgical prayer for God's forgiveness that we pray before Communion includes both the things we have done and the things we have left undone. Inaction, silence, and indifference are also relational failures. They breed injustice, oppression, and death.

Dominique DuBois Gilliard is the director of racial righteousness and reconciliation for the Love Mercy Do Justice initiative of the Evangelical Covenant Church. An ordained minister, he previously served in pastoral ministry in Oakland, Chicago, and Atlanta. He serves on the board of directors for the Christian Community Development Association (CCDA) and Evangelicals for Justice.

TESTED BY THE EVIL TRICKSTER

²For forty days and nights Creator Sets Free (Jesus) ate nothing. *His body became weak*, and his hunger grew strong.

³*When* the evil snake *saw that Creator Sets Free (Jesus) was weak and hungry, he* came to him *and whispered in his ear.*

"Are you the Son of the Great Spirit?" he hissed. "Prove it by turning these stones into frybread."

⁴"The Sacred Teachings are clear," Creator Sets Free (Jesus) said. "Human beings cannot live only on frybread, but on all the words that come from the mouth of the Great Spirit."ᵃ

⁵The evil trickster then took him to the Great Spirit's sacred lodge in Village of Peace (Jerusalem). He set him at the very top, *high above the village.*

⁶"Prove you are the Son of the Great Spirit and jump down from here!" the evil snake taunted him. "Do not the Sacred Teachings also say, 'His spirit-messengers will watch over you to keep you from harm. They will even keep your foot from hitting a stone'ᵇ?"

⁷"Yes," Creator Sets Free (Jesus) said back to him, "but they also say, 'Do not test the Great Spirit.'ᶜ"

⁸Once more the evil trickster took him to a high mountain and showed him all the great nations of the world with their power and beauty.

[9]"All of these I will give you," the snake said *smoothly*, "if you will highly honor me and walk in my ways!"

[10]"Get away from me, Accuser (Satan)!" he responded. "For it is written in the Sacred Teachings, 'The Great Spirit is the only one to honor and serve.'[d]"

MATTHEW 4:2-10 FNV

Terry M. Wildman is the lead translator, general editor, and project manager of the *First Nations Version*. He is the founder of Rain Ministries and serves as the director of spiritual growth and leadership development for Native InterVarsity. He and his wife, Darlene, live in Arizona.

BREATH PRAYER

BREATHE IN

*Blessed are those
who hunger.*

BREATHE OUT

They will be filled.

INVOLUNTARY FASTING

MARLENA GRAVES, *THE WAY UP IS DOWN*

Blessed are those who hunger and thirst for
righteousness, for they will be filled.

MATTHEW 5:6

When God is silent and darkness covers the face of my earth, I just take a number and stand in a long line with the rest of them—Job, Jesus, and all those throughout millennia who've had God plead the Fifth on them. My greatest of tantrums, most brilliant protests, and intestine-twisting agonies seldom pry a straight answer or any answer at all out of him when I want one.

Even though I think I know that, after so long I find I am unable to wait anymore in the waiting room of life. So, I shoot up from the chair and try a different tactic. I pace back and forth like a caged animal. Stomp on the floor. Make all the noise I can. Wave my hands like a fool trying different antics to get God's attention. When that doesn't work, I head straight to God's door and start asking, seeking, and knocking. No, *pounding*. "I know you're in there. When you gonna show your face?" I figure I'll be the persistent widow. But God persists in responding in his own time, in his own way, and on his own terms. I am forced to sit down again, to trust him instead of giving in to despair while he has the right to remain silent. I can't stand it. Most of the time I can only trust him in the new round of waiting with the help of others. On my own, I fall apart. And yet even the waiting room of my life remains God-haunted. Really, what I am is God-intoxicated, a staggering drunk.

My daily and desperate need for him and the physical hunger I sometimes experienced as a child—emptiness—was sort of an involuntary fast. It all coalesced into my constant awareness of the manifest presence of God, into his always being on my mind, ever before me. And yet, on some days, I still find myself empty. I do things like read God the riot act and insinuate his betrayal. How can this be?

I don't know.

Just like I don't know how Satan could have turned from God. Or how Adam and Eve could've sinned when they had everything they could have ever wanted in God. Or how Judas could've betrayed Jesus after spending three years with him. Or how Peter betrayed Jesus to his face shortly after promising he never would.

What if I, like Adam, Eve, Judas, and Peter, have everything I could possibly ever want right now in God and just don't see what is right in front of me? What if I am refusing to see it?

Marlena Graves is a writer, adjunct professor at Winebrenner Theological Seminary, and author of *A Beautiful Disaster* and *Forty Days on Being a Nine.* She holds an MDiv from Northeastern Seminary in Rochester, New York, and is working on her PhD in American Cultural Studies at Bowling Green State University.

. . . .

LOVING INTERRUPTION

JOHN PERKINS, *WELCOMING JUSTICE*

*This is my commandment, that you love
one another as I have loved you.*

JOHN 15:12

Jesus is the incarnation of God's love. "He himself is our peace," Ephesians 2:14 says (NIV). But Jesus also said he came into our world to disturb the peace—to drive a wedge into the divided society that holds us captive. "Do not suppose that I have come to bring peace to the earth," he says in Matthew's Gospel. "I did not come to bring peace, but a sword" (Matthew 10:34 NIV). That sword is a wedge to interrupt the way things are, not a weapon to wield in defense of the status quo. Instead of continually seeking God's will for our lives and communities, we hold the Holy Spirit captive to our own desires—our selfish, materialistic desires. We see this in the prosperity gospel running rampant through the church today. The church is called to be the prophetic voice in response to society; that's what we see in the model Jesus provided.

I believe God interrupts us with his love. So often when we're interrupted, we get mad. I know what it feels like to be mad at God. When my son Spencer died, I was mad at God. Spencer had given his whole life to reconciliation, and I was so proud of him.

I prayed and said, "God, Spencer was a reconciler. He gave his life trying to bridge the racial divide in this country. I've been saying you took him, Lord, but he laid down his life willingly for you. And I want to release him. I want to give him back to you, God." I said that prayer and knew that God had interrupted me with his love. God showed me through Spencer's death that I needed to give the rest of my life to reconciliation right here in West Jackson where Spencer was trying to do it. Whatever the cost, I needed to carry on the work that he'd been called to do.

His work was the same work Paul had been called to on the Damascus Road: the work of proclaiming reconciliation for all people in Jesus Christ. From the very beginning of God's movement in the world, God has been interrupting people with his love—disturbing our false peace in order to make real peace possible. Jesus drives a wedge in the status quo to create space for something new. If we have ears to hear, the invitation is open for each of us: come and be part of the beloved community that God makes possible in Jesus Christ.

John Perkins is the founder of Voice of Calvary Ministries in Mendenhall, Mississippi; Harambee Ministries in Pasadena, California; and the Christian Community Development Association. He coauthored *Welcoming Justice* with Charles Marsh and his other books include *Let Justice Roll Down*, *With Justice for All*, and *Making Neighborhoods Whole*.

. . . .

HANDS FULL OF HEAVEN

DREW JACKSON, *GOD SPEAKS THROUGH WOMBS*

> *Then he looked up at his disciples and said:*
> *"Blessed are you who are poor,*
> *for yours is the kingdom of God."*

LUKE 6:20

Hands held out.
The bottom edges pressed together,
making the shape of a metacarpus cup.

Nothing in them
except the air of aspiration,
anticipating grace from passersby.

I never miss
the gifts that heaven drops.
The crumbs from this table are decadent.

These people rushing by me
to arrive at their importance
miss so many riches.

Their hands
full of briefcases
and ambition.

I will take all the heaven
I can gather for today.
Tomorrow I will sit,

again,
with these hands cupped
to receive my enough.

Drew Jackson is the founding pastor of Hope East Village in New York City. He also writes poetry at the intersection of justice, peace, and contemplation, with a passion to contribute toward a more just and whole world. He and his wife have twin daughters and live in Lower Manhattan.

EMPTYING TO RECEIVE

JOSHUA CHOONMIN KANG, *DEEP-ROOTED IN CHRIST*

Humble yourselves therefore under the mighty hand
of God, so that he may exalt you in due time.

1 PETER 5:6

Most of us long for transformation but are afraid to change. Yet spiritual formation begins when we empty our lives. Our spiritual formation begins not with fullness but with emptiness. That's the way we follow Jesus, who "emptied himself, taking the form of a slave, being born in human likeness" (Philippians 2:7).

Even Jesus had to make space for God's action in his life. He had a privileged status, but he relinquished it; he let it go. It's the same with us. We have to empty ourselves. Only then can we begin to be filled up with the blessings of God.

What do we mean by emptying ourselves? How can we connect with this need to give ourselves away?

Let's look first at the figure of Abraham. Abraham began by departing, by leaving home in response to God's command. His departure wasn't just a matter of location. He had to abandon whatever he knew best: his safe haven, his comfort zone.

This is what God is asking us to do as well. He wants us to let go of our old country and enter into the new life he has in mind for us. But abandoning our comfort zones can be terrifying. When we let go of the world we know, we're going to experience pain, suffering, and fear.

Many of us who are Korean know what it is like to leave a homeland. We know our own stories and those of others, describing what it is to leave the place we knew best. What a land journey we've made! But our *spiritual* journey isn't only geographic. It's much more than traveling in time and space.

Departing isn't only a matter of location. It's not just leaving one place to go to another. The letting go takes place in the spiritual realm. That is where the deeper journey is made. This deeper journey is a life-passage of abandonment: letting go of our old ways to find the new; emptying ourselves as preparation for receiving the grace God will pour into us.

 **Joshua Choonmin Kang** is founding pastor of New Life Vision Church in the Koreatown area of Los Angeles, California. He is also the author of *Spirituality of Gratitude* and *Scripture by Heart*. Kang has written thirty books in Korean, including *God's Grace That Turns the Life Around*.

HE TALKS TO THE ANCESTORS

¹Six days later, Creator Sets Free (Jesus) took *only* Stands on the Rock (Peter), He Takes Over (James), and his brother He Shows Goodwill (John) up on a great high mountain. ²Right there before them his appearance began to change. His clothes turned bright white, and his face began to shine like the sun.

³Then before their eyes *two ancestors appeared—the lawgiver* Drawn from the Water (Moses) and *the ancient prophet* Great Spirit Is Creator (Elijah). They were talking with Creator Sets Free (Jesus).

They all stared in wide-eyed wonder, not knowing what to say. Then Stands on the Rock (Peter) found his voice.

⁴"Wisdomkeeper," he said out loud, "this is a good place to stay. If you want, I will put up three tipis—one for you, one for Drawn from the Water (Moses), and one for Great Spirit Is Creator (Elijah)."

⁵While he was still speaking, a bright cloud covered them. A voice spoke from the cloud, saying, "This is my much-loved Son, the one who makes my heart glad. Listen to him!"

⁶They all fell on their faces in fear, ⁷but Creator Sets Free (Jesus) laid his hands on them and said, "Do not fear! Stand to your feet."

MATTHEW 17:1-7 FNV

. . . .

GOD'S SUPPLY

DONNA BARBER, *BREAD FOR THE RESISTANCE*

And God is able to make all grace abound toward
you; that ye, always having all sufficiency in all
things, may abound to every good work.

2 CORINTHIANS 9:8 KJV

Emptying myself before the Father is a necessary and re-curring step in my discipleship journey. Of my own free will, I approach the altar of God. I lay down all of me as a yielded sacrifice. My body, my mind, my gifts and talents, my posses-sions, my time, my relationships, my future, my hopes and dreams and desires and imagination—I lay it all at his feet in response to the immense gift of life I have received from him. It is not until I am spent, completely empty of myself, that I am ready to serve others.

We cannot serve from our own wealth, no matter how great, for it will soon be depleted. If we attempt to give to others out of our own supply, our generosity can quickly deteriorate into paternalism, or become tainted by the impure motives of power and control, or weighted with the expectation of reci-procity. No, we must give out of the resources of heaven that we access when we enter the quiet space of worship and prayer—the holy of holies. There, as we stand before the throne of his greatness, we remember the truth. Then we can open our empty hands, heart, and mind before him and be filled.

Over the years we are often prompted to open our lives to others, to make room in our homes, work, or schedules for strangers and friends. We share time and family, business contacts and date nights, holidays and influence, speaker platforms and food. We move through the world like I imagine the disciples wading through the hungry crowds, marveling at God's provision. We close our eyes in prayer over bread crumbs and scraps of fish. He sends us out with hands and baskets nearly empty. Our bodies get tired and our feet grow sore from the journey. Yet moving at his command, every step taken and every item shared brings God-given grace. And we soon realize we have even more to give.

When we begin at empty, we are forced to work from God's supply, according to his timetable and at his pace. We are more often unseen and may go unappreciated, but we are seldom burned out. Instead we are emptied again and again, forced to return to our source to be refilled of his grace and power, and sustained by his infinite love. When we first give our whole selves to him without coercion, then our sacrifices, no matter how great or how many, seem quite small.

Donna Barber is cofounder of The Voices Project, an organization that influences culture through training and promoting leaders of color. She is also director of Champions Academy, an initiative providing culturally responsive leadership development for student athletes. She lives in Portland, Oregon, with her husband, Leroy, and their children.

BREATH PRAYER

BREATHE IN

God is able.

BREATHE OUT

To make all grace abound.

TRANSPARENCY

NATASHA SISTRUNK ROBINSON,
A SOJOURNER'S TRUTH

*And all of us, with unveiled faces, seeing the glory
of the Lord as though reflected in a mirror, are being
transformed into the same image from one degree of glory
to another; for this comes from the Lord, the Spirit.*

2 CORINTHIANS 3:18

Loving yourself means being honest with God and others about your struggles. Through my wilderness experiences, I have discovered that the people I love need to see the real me with an unveiled face. They don't have to always understand, but they do need to see the glow when I experience the glory of the God, without me wondering if that brightness is going to blind them. And I need to speak honestly when that light starts to dim without wondering if the Lord has left us (see Exodus 34:29-35). We need not be afraid. God touches us in the darkness and in the light.

Transparency is healing. Being transparent is the only way we can allow others to take the redemptive journey with us. Nouwen reminds us that "laying down [our lives] means making [our] own faith and doubt, hope and despair, joy and sadness, courage and fear available to others as ways of getting in touch with the Lord of life." Staying connected to God is something we learn to do together. We especially need this support when we have gone through a dark place, when we are taking a new journey, or when we don't know where we are going or what to do.

I remember sitting in the bed next to my husband. We were trying to rebuild a marriage that was broken.

I wanted to heal and I wanted us to heal. I wanted to become a peacemaker and not a "peace faker." Yet the healing did not come for us individually or collectively until we truly confessed our sins to God and to each other, until we replaced the lies we had accepted and believed about the other with the truth of how God wants us to become his agents of grace for each other, and until we repented of the old way. Our healing began when we decided that we were not each other's enemies, but we were going to work and get better together.

I can't be a true peacemaker alone, and I could not sustain the holy ministry of marriage alone. Trusting God and going at it together relieves a lot of the burden of our brokenness, and it requires that we care for each other on the way.

 **Natasha Sistrunk Robinson** is an international speaker, leadership consultant, mentoring coach, and the visionary founder of the nonprofit Leadership LINKS, Inc. A graduate of the US Naval Academy and a former Marine Corps officer, she is author of *Mentor for Life* and *Hope for Us*.

RETURNING TO SHALOM TOGETHER

DAN STRINGER, *STRUGGLING WITH EVANGELICALISM*

*I have come to call not the righteous
but sinners to repentance.*

LUKE 5:32

Scripture is packed with descriptions of repentance and instructions stressing its importance. There is no sinner's prayer without admitting that you're a sinner. Repentance is foundational to discipleship. Jesus starts his ministry with a call to repentance. Following his temptation by the devil in the wilderness, Jesus begins preaching with the words, "Repent, for the kingdom of heaven has come near" (Matthew 4:17 NIV). Right out of the gate, Jesus draws a connection between repentance and the kingdom of heaven.

When the very first Christian church was launched in Jerusalem, the apostle Peter preached a sermon explaining the significance of Jesus' life, death, and resurrection. After hearing this message, the people were cut to the heart and asked Peter and the other apostles, "What shall we do?" Peter began his reply this way: "Repent and be baptized, every one of you, in the name of Jesus Christ for the forgiveness of your sins" (Acts 2:37-38 NIV). Attempting to follow Jesus without repentance is like trying to play solitaire without knowing what a deck of cards is. There's no discipleship without repentance.

The answer depends on what is being asked. If we're talking about placing one's trust in Jesus, that would be one thing. It's easy to see the importance of repentance for personal salvation. But if we're asking why repentance matters to evangelicalism as a shared space, the question becomes one about collective repentance. Is it possible for evangelicalism to repent collectively? If we did, what would that even look like?

Individual sins certainly matter, but they aren't the only sins that matter. Individualism says, "The sins of others aren't my fault," but collective repentance is a longstanding biblical practice for God's people. Collective sins require collective repentance. Until we acknowledge how we have fractured shalom with God, neighbor, and creation, we cannot begin to make right what has gone wrong. Individuals pray a sinner's prayer, but the church prays a sinners' prayer.

Dan Stringer is ordained in the Evangelical Covenant Church and serves as team leader for InterVarsity's Graduate and Faculty Ministries in Hawai'i. He is pastor of theological formation at Wellspring Covenant Church in Hālawa, Hawai'i.

MYSTERIOUS NOURISHMENT

TISH HARRISON WARREN, *LITURGY OF THE ORDINARY*

I am the living bread that came down from heaven.

JOHN 6:51

The Eucharist is a profoundly communal meal that reorients us from people who are merely individualistic consumers into people who are, together, capable of imaging Christ in the world. Of course, eating itself reminds us that none of us can stay alive on our own. If you are breathing, it's because someone fed you. In this way the act of eating reorients us from an atomistic, independent existence toward one that is interdependent. But the Eucharist goes even further. In it, we feast on Christ, and are thereby mysteriously formed together into one body, the body of Christ.

Nourishment is always far more than biological nutrition. We are nourished by our communities. We are nourished by gratitude. We are nourished by justice. We are nourished when we know and love our neighbors.

This "global theology" of consumerism has transformed both the way we eat and the way we worship. The evangelical quest for a particular emotional experience in worship and the capitalistic quest for anonymous, cheap canned goods have something in common. Both are mostly concerned with what I can get for myself, as an individual consumer.

But the economy of the Eucharist calls me to a life of self-emptying worship.

We must guard against those practices—both in the church and in our daily life—that shape us into mere consumers. Spirituality packaged as a path to personal self-fulfillment and happiness fits neatly into Western consumerism. But the Scriptures and the sacraments reorient us into people who feed on the Bread of Life together and are sent out as stewards of redemption.

We are formed by our habits of consumption.

And in contemporary America, this daily formation is often at odds with our formation in Word and sacrament. In this alternative economy of the true Bread of Life, we are turned inside out so that we are no longer people marked by scarcity, jockeying for our own good, but are new people, truly nourished, and therefore able to extend nourishment to others. The economy of the Eucharist is true abundance. There is enough for me, not in spite of others, but because we receive Christ together as a community.

Tish Harrison Warren is a weekly contributing newsletter writer for the *New York Times* and writes a monthly column for *Christianity Today*. She is a writer in residence at Resurrection South Austin, a priest in the Anglican Church in North America, and a senior fellow with The Trinity Forum.

BREATH PRAYER

BREATHE IN

Heal the brokenhearted.

BREATHE OUT

Bind up our wounds.

SET FREE FROM BROKEN WAYS

[6]When the time was right, while we were still weak human beings following our bad hearts and broken ways, the Chosen One died for us. [7]It is not easy to find someone who is willing to die for a good person, even though we might find someone with the courage to die for a very good person. [8]But here is the way the Maker of Life proves how deep his love is for us: even when we were still following our bad hearts and broken ways, the Chosen One gave his life for us. [9]The lifeblood that he poured out puts our lives back into harmony and promises us good standing with the Great Spirit. What he has done sets us free from the storm of great anger caused by our bad hearts and broken ways.

[10]So, if the lifeblood poured out by the Chosen One has put us in good standing with the Great Spirit, then how much more will his life of beauty and harmony, which has defeated death, now set us free to walk in his ways!

[11]But taking this a step further, we can now boast with glad hearts about what the Great Spirit has done through our Honored Chief Creator Sets Free (Jesus) the Chosen One! He is the one who has restored us back into friendship with the Great Spirit!

ROMANS 5:6-11 FNV

RECOVERING IN COMMUNITY

GRACE JI-SUN KIM AND GRAHAM HILL, *HEALING OUR BROKEN HUMANITY*

*By this everyone will know that you are my
disciples, if you have love for one another.*

JOHN 13:35

Christianity's challenge isn't relating (or being relevant) to a secular and consumerist age. It's seeing how much Christianity is now secularized, consumerist, and assimilated, and then choosing to resist and to pursue another way. In *A Way Other Than Our Own*, Walter Brueggemann says, "The crisis in the [American] church has almost nothing to do with being liberal or conservative; it has everything to do with giving up on the faith and discipline of our Christian baptism and settling for a common, generic [American] identity that is part patriotism, part consumerism, part violence, and part affluence."

The world needs persons, families, and communities that show the power of simplicity and contentment. We can't be people of both light and darkness, faith and greed, love and distrust, or God and money. Our society often tempts us to long for power, lust for sex, trust in violence, believe in the nation-state, and yearn for affluence and wealth. But we can't worship two gods at once.

The gods of technology, media, patriotism, sex, consumerism, the stock market, violence, guns, and affluence are never satisfied. Once they have secured your worship, they demand your entire life. But Jesus calls us to recover a life of God worship together. Different values and desires shape this new life together: love, simplicity, contentment, nonviolence, and membership in Jesus' *kin-dom*. This is a radical social ethic. This is a dangerous way of life together in the world. It disrupts and confronts the status quo. It's as startling and dangerous today as it was in Jesus' time.

Grace Ji-Sun Kim is associate professor of theology at Earlham School of Religion. Her books include *Embracing the Other, Christian Doctrines for Global Gender Justice*, and *Intercultural Ministry*. She is an ordained minister in the Presbyterian Church (USA).

Graham Hill is research coordinator at Stirling Theological College in Melbourne. A former church planter, he is the founding director of theglobalchurchproject.com. His books include *GlobalChurch* and *Salt, Light, and a City*.

LIVING WORSHIP

MARK E. STRONG, *DIVINE MERGER*

Do not conform to the pattern of this world,
but be transformed by the renewing of your mind.
Then you will be able to test and approve what God's
will is—his good, pleasing and perfect will.

ROMANS 12:2 NIV

An altar is a place of interaction between the God of heaven and a man or woman on earth. It's the meeting place where a merger is forged between the heart of God and the heart of the worshiper.

You can't have an altar without a sacrifice. Jesus is the ultimate sacrifice for us; he has already paid the price for us by giving his life. However, each of us can also offer our lives to God in love, adoration, and service toward him.

I heard a story about a little boy who wanted to give God an offering but had nothing to give. He sat on the floor, watching people pass by and place their offerings in large wicker baskets. How he longed to give a little something to the Savior he so dearly loved. He walked to the front of the church, grabbed the rim of the basket and hoisted himself inside. When the deacons went to retrieve the boy, one scolded him, saying, "This is not a play area!" Embarrassed and bewildered, the little boy responded, "I didn't have anything to give the Lord, so I was giving him myself."

The altar of our heart is where we can put our entire being in the offering basket and say to the Lord, "Jesus, I am giving you all of me." Out of that loving surrender to the Master, God can put your life in the place where you are supposed to be. Romans 12:1-2 tells us how to climb into in the basket.

Friend, you are not just *anything*, you are *something*. As they say in the country, "You're something mighty special!" So, what are you waiting for? Climb in the basket and offer yourself totally to God by worshiping him with all you are. He will use your life beyond your wildest dreams and imaginations.

Mark E. Strong is senior pastor of Life Change Church, a diverse congregation in the heart of inner-city Portland, Oregon. He is author of *Church for the Fatherless,* founder of Father-Shift, and serves on the Board of Regents at George Fox Seminary. He and his wife, Marla, have four children.

WEEK THREE, SATURDAY

. . . .

CARE FOR THE WEARY

SHEILA WISE ROWE, *HEALING RACIAL TRAUMA*

> *You will keep in perfect peace*
> *those whose minds are steadfast,*
> *because they trust in you.*

ISAIAH 26:3 NIV

Soul care should be holistic, involving our spiritual, emotional, relational, physical, and vocational lives. When you are engaging in healthy soul care, you know when and how to rest, de-stress, expose injustice, and advocate for your needs and those of others. Old practices that helped our ancestors to cope and heal have been discarded; we should now reengage them. All of these help us to build resilience. It's also time to develop methods of soul care that builds on the past, the present, and our resilience, and recognizes that in Christ we are and have more than enough.

When you are distracted and flat in your connection to the Lord, it is a warning sign that something is off. Have you had an experience that has caused a moral injury? Has it caused you to question the goodness of God? If this is the case, your relationship with God may be affected and in need of soul

41

repair. Soul repair begins as you prioritize your relationship with the Lord, not just to share what's on your heart but also to hear what is on his. It also helps to regularly read the Scriptures and other inspirational books. When you take a sabbath day of rest each week, it is an act of trust to set aside your work and fear and place them in God's capable hands while you rest. When you are attentive to the Lord your perspective becomes clearer, fear is reduced, and you're less likely to get caught up in unnecessary drama. It is essential that you worship from your heart; do not relegate your culture to the margins. Worship and pray in your own language and in your own ways. During slavery, Negro spirituals like "Wade in the Water" were thought to be solely about water baptism, but it was a song of faith, perseverance, hope, and freedom.

Sheila Wise Rowe holds a master's degree in counseling psychology and has ministered to abuse and trauma survivors in the United States and Johannesburg, South Africa. She is the cofounder of The Cyrene Movement and a writer, counselor, speaker, and spiritual director in the Boston area.

· · · · · · · · · · · · · · ·

SEEKING JUSTICE

BETHANY H. HOANG, *DEEPENING THE SOUL FOR JUSTICE*

But strive first for the kingdom of God and his righteousness, and all these things will be given to you as well.

MATTHEW 6:33

Seeking justice begins with seeking the God of justice. The difference between a pursuit of justice that brings transformation for real people suffering real violence and a pursuit of justice that amounts to little more than good intentions is simple—perhaps even simpler than we want it to be. The difference is found at our starting point, every single day.

Fighting injustice—the abuse of power that oppresses the vulnerable through violence and lies—can be excruciatingly hard work. It can be exhausting. It is relentless. But Jesus offers to make our burdens light, even the burden of fighting injustice.

And so, seeking justice—bringing right order and exerting life-giving power to protect the vulnerable—does not begin at the threshold of abuse. Seeking justice begins with seeking God: our God who longs to bring justice; our God who longs to use *us*, every one of his children, to bring justice; our God who offers us the yoke of Jesus in exchange for things that otherwise leave us defeated.

At the end of the day, if our attempts to seek justice do not first begin with the work of prayer, we will be worn and weary. And our weariness will not be that deeply satisfying, joy-filled tiredness that comes from the worthy battles of justice, but rather a bone- and soul-crushing weariness.

But when the work of justice is pursued first, and throughout, as a work of prayer and an outpouring of our relationship with Jesus Christ, obstacles become opportunities to know the riches of God's glory and great presence in ever-increasing measure.

We might know in our heads that prayer and other spiritual disciplines matter, but more than likely we pursue prayer more as a halfhearted occasional duty rather than as the God-given relationship and power undergirding and fueling all of our action. Or perhaps we view it as much more relevant to our personal spiritual growth and the issues and pain we see in the lives of those closest to us—not the pain and mind-boggling complexity of millions who suffer injustice in the world. And yet this great power and source of intimacy with God is what God intends prayer to be in our lives, in every area of mission to which God calls us.

Bethany H. Hoang is the director of the International Justice Mission (IJM) Institute for Biblical Justice. Since joining IJM in 2004, she has traveled globally, teaching thousands at churches, conferences, and universities. She is responsible for equipping leaders of the global church and academic communities with resources to seek justice.

BREATH PRAYER

BREATHE IN

Lord Jesus Christ.

BREATHE OUT

Draw near to me.

I WAS BLIND BUT NOW I SEE

²⁴They went back to the man who was blind and said to him, "Give honor to the Great Spirit for healing you, not to Creator Sets Free (Jesus), for we know he is an outcast with a bad heart."

²⁵"I do not know whether this man has a bad heart," he answered them. "But this I do know—I was blind but now I see."

²⁶They asked the man again, "What did he do to open your eyes?"

²⁷He said to them, "You did not listen the first time I told you. Why do you want to hear it again? Do you also want to become one of his followers?"

This made the leaders angry, so they tried to insult the man.

²⁸"You are his follower!" they said with disrespect in their voices. "We follow Drawn from the Water (Moses), ²⁹for we know the Great Spirit has spoken to him, but we do not know where this man is from."

³⁰The man answered them, "This is a strange thing! You, who are tribal leaders, do not know where this man comes from, yet he is the one who opened my eyes. ³¹The Great Spirit does not listen to people with bad hearts. He listens to the ones who humbly serve him and do what is right. ³²From the creation of the world no one has ever seen a man healed who was born blind. ³³If he were not from the Great Spirit, he could not have done this."

JOHN 9:24-33 FNV

DISSOLVED BARRIERS

GREGORY COLES, *NO LONGER STRANGERS*

For in him the whole fullness of deity dwells bodily.

COLOSSIANS 2:9

Emmanuel, Jesus is called. God with us. God in proximity to us.

If Jesus treated proximity the way I so often do, his incarnation wouldn't have been so scandalous an event. He could have made his appearance on earth with a polite degree of removal, like a benevolent monarch condescending to visit the countryside for an afternoon, like a doctor with blue nitrile gloves and a face mask stepping into the patient's room only as long as necessary. He could have placed himself in a different silo of humanity than the rest of us are in. (If anyone deserves a silo of humanity all to themselves, it's Jesus. Beyoncé might also merit such a silo, but only secondarily and for less theological reasons.)

Instead, Jesus had a habit of touching others and allowing them to touch him—even the lepers and known miscreants, the people whose physical and spiritual maladies could have repulsed him. He attended house parties not just with the tax collectors who expected to be judged by him, but also with the Pharisees who took great delight in judging him. He sought out disciples who were wildly different from him and from each other, disciples who would never have sat at the same table with one another in a high school cafeteria.

Jesus didn't abide by anyone else's silos. Young or old, rich or beggar, healthy or bleeding, holy or heinous, Brahmin or Untouchable—the boundaries all dissolved in his company. No one was left lingering under the shade of a banana tree, because neither superiority nor inferiority had the power to keep anyone isolated. Jesus descended from the highest possible place, crushing each rung of the ladder on his way down, until he was proximate to the lowest people he could find.

He is the God who stays, the God who claims us as his own, the God who refuses to be shoved out of the way, even when we begin to bleed on him. He is the God who says, "Let me take all your burdens and make them mine. Let me bleed instead."

Emmanuel makes our proximity into something sacred.

 **Gregory Coles** is a writer, speaker, and worship leader. His first book, *Single, Gay, Christian*, was a 2017 Foreword INDIES Award Finalist. He lives in central Pennsylvania, where he recently completed a PhD in English from Penn State.

HOLISTIC HARMONY

BRENDA SALTER McNEIL, *A CREDIBLE WITNESS*

*In him the whole structure is joined together and grows
into a holy temple in the Lord; in whom you also are built
together spiritually into a dwelling place for God.*

EPHESIANS 2:21

On the cross Jesus reconciled us to God, and he also reconciled us to each other—both in the same act of salvation. Because of the death and resurrection of Jesus Christ, there are no divisions or barriers that separate us from God or from each other. To choose Christ is also to choose his community. According to Ephesians 2, Jesus died so that we could have peace with God *and* with each other. As a result of his heroic sacrifice we are now members of God's family—a new, blood-related people group. Men and women, girls and boys, the young and the old, people from different social classes, ethnic backgrounds, and religious traditions have been reconciled and are now of the same household.

This is the whole truth of the gospel. It is an unusual and especially compelling truth in a world that is marked by war, broken relationships, racial and ethnic strife, and economic divisions. When people see us living out the reality of being one multiethnic, multilingual, multicultural, and multinational family in Christ, it grabs their attention, piques their curiosity and causes them to wonder what makes us this way. It is what Jesus called us to do in Matthew 5:16 when he said, "Let your light shine before others, so that they may see your good works and give glory to your Father in heaven." A corporate witness to the reality of reconciliation is a perfect demonstration of the gospel. Our unity in the midst of our diversity is one of the most powerful ways we reveal the reality of what Jesus accomplished on the cross.

It's a shame that Christians have been evangelized without hearing the whole message of the gospel, which says that God is not mad at us, that all barriers that have divided us from God and from each other have been destroyed and that we are now representatives of the kingdom, which is composed of people from every tribe, language, and nation.

 **Brenda Salter McNeil** is a dynamic speaker, author, and trailblazer with over thirty years of experience in the ministry of racial, ethnic, and gender reconciliation. She is an associate professor of reconciliation studies in the School of Theology at Seattle Pacific University. She is also the coauthor of *The Heart of Racial Justice* and author of *Roadmap to Reconciliation*.

AT THE TABLE

SANDRA MARIA VAN OPSTAL, *THE NEXT WORSHIP*

For all who exalt themselves will be humbled, and
those who humble themselves will be exalted.

LUKE 14:11

In worship, as we interact in community, connecting with one another, we encounter God. If the worship experience and practice is filled with people coming from different ethnic backgrounds, social ranks and ways of eating, then there will be opportunity to enjoy God's presence together. This guiding image of communion at the Table of Christ is central to why we participate in crosscultural worship. The table communicates fellowship with others (across differences, as Jesus modeled) and with God.

One of my favorite places to encounter Christ at the table is in Luke 14, which illustrates a master's invitation to a great banquet feast. The master's invitation list reveals no favoritism at the table. All are invited to the banquet: the social elite as well as those from the highways and byways. The tension mounts: when people from different ethnic and socioeconomic standings gather, the result is awkward dinner conversations. And let's face it, we tend to avoid parties where we expect awkwardness.

But isn't being at the Lord's Table in the church like being at an awkward party? Imagine a dinner where random strangers from all walks of life—poor, rich, old, young—are invited. There they are, staring at one another across the table wondering what they can possibly say and why the other is dressed like *that*. This is the church! The church consists of people from *every* walk of life, profession, culture, nationality, race, and background. We come together at God's invitation. The table is an intimate and unique place of communion; shouldn't we Christians be able to share a meal without the painful moments of disconnect? It would be easy if we were all clones, but God in his wisdom did not create us that way. As individuals we are different, and as communities we are different.

Sandra Maria Van Opstal is an activist and second-generation Latina pastor. She is the author of *The Mission of Worship* and *Forty Days on Being an Eight*. She is executive director of Chasing Justice, a movement that mobilizes Christians to live justly. Sandra is currently pursuing doctoral work in urban leadership and transformation.

COMPANIONS ON
THE JOURNEY

RUTH HALEY BARTON, *LIFE TOGETHER IN CHRIST*

Was it not necessary that the Messiah should suffer
these things and then enter into his glory?

LUKE 24:26

Peter's (and presumably the other disciples') difficulty accepting the fact that Jesus would have to suffer raises a sobering possibility for spiritual companions to consider, and it is this: in our attempts to be loyal and faithful and helpful (as Peter was surely trying to be), we too could be a distraction and even a stumbling block to one another if we fail to understand the nature of the spiritual journey and God's divine purposes in all aspects of the journey, including suffering. How confusing it can be if members of a spiritual community have fundamentally different ideas about what the spiritual journey is all about.

For instance, if one's vision of the journey is shaped by a "success gospel" in which the sign of God's blessing is that everything is always "up and to the right" while others understand it to be a series of "necessary deaths" in which we let go of that which is false so what is truest within us can fully emerge, we could actually do more harm than good in our attempts to companion one another! If some in the group believe that growth in the spiritual life is marked by increasing certitude while others are being drawn into the kinds of questions that defy easy answers and trite sayings, we could actually thwart what God is trying to do in their lives.

One of the most valuable offerings we can make to one another in transforming community is the perspective that enables us to "see through" to what is really going on spiritually speaking, no matter how painful the events and experiences might be. To affirm that God is at work even in our suffering can be redemptive if we allow it to be.

This necessary rhythm of suffering and death, burial and resurrection was the *spiritual* reality Jesus' disciples were living through in a condensed fashion as they experienced the events of that first "Good" Friday, waited numbly through that first Holy Saturday, and tried to find their way back home on that first Resurrection Sunday. Even though they hadn't been able to make sense of it yet, Jesus' journey from death to life was revealing the true nature of the spiritual life. And as he interpreted the events of the previous days, he was signaling to them that we too must "die" if we desire to be raised to new life in Christ. We, too, must lay down *anything* that is a hindrance to us spiritually, so we can walk in newness of life.

Ruth Haley Barton is founder of the Transforming Center, a ministry dedicated to strengthening the souls of pastors and Christian leaders, and the congregations and organizations they serve. Her books include *Strengthening the Soul of Your Leadership*, *Pursuing God's Will Together*, and *Invitation to Retreat*.

BREATH PRAYER

BREATHE IN

I (or we) believe.

BREATHE OUT

Life is in you.

....

FOUR DAYS DEAD

¹⁷When Creator Sets Free (Jesus) came to House of Figs (Bethany), he found out that Creator Helps Him (Lazarus) had died four days earlier and was laid in a burial cave.

¹⁹Many of the local Tribal Members had gathered, along with the women, to give comfort to Head Woman (Martha) and Healing Tears (Mary) for the loss of their brother.

I AM THE RISING FROM THE DEAD

²⁰When Head Woman (Martha) heard that Creator Sets Free (Jesus) was coming, she went out to greet him, but Healing Tears (Mary) stayed home.

²¹When she found Creator Sets Free (Jesus), she said to him, "Wisdomkeeper, if you had been here, my brother would still be with us. ²²Even so, I know if you ask anything of the Great Spirit, he will give it to you."

²³"Your brother will live again," he answered.

²⁴"I know he will live again," she said, "when the dead rise up at the end of all days."

²⁵⁻²⁶"I am the rising from the dead and the life that follows," he told her. "The ones who trust me will live again, even after death. Death will never be the end of the ones who are alive and trust in me. Do you believe what I am saying to you?"

²⁷"Yes, Wisdomkeeper!" she *smiled and* said. "I believe you are the Chosen One, the Son of the Great Spirit—the one who came *down* into this world *from above*."

JOHN 11:17, 19-27 FNV

THE DEPTHS

**EUGENE H. PETERSON, *A LONG OBEDIENCE
IN THE SAME DIRECTION***

> *Help, GOD—I've hit rock bottom!*
> *Master, hear my cry for help!*
> *Listen hard! Open your ears!*
> *Listen to my cries for mercy.*

PSALM 130:1-2 *THE MESSAGE*

By setting the anguish out in the open and voicing it as a prayer, the psalm gives dignity to our suffering. It does not look on suffering as something slightly embarrassing that must be hushed up and locked in a closet (where it finally becomes a skeleton) because this sort of thing shouldn't happen to a real person of faith. And it doesn't treat it as a puzzle that must be explained, and therefore turn it over to theologians or philosophers to work out an answer. Suffering is set squarely, openly, passionately before God. It is acknowledged and expressed. It is described and lived.

If the psalm did nothing more than that, it would be a prize, for it is difficult to find anyone in our culture who will respect us when we suffer. We live in a time when everyone's goal is to be perpetually healthy and constantly happy. If any one of us fails to live up to the standards that are advertised as normative, we are labeled as a problem to be solved, and a host of well-intentioned people rush to try out various cures on us. Or we are looked on as an enigma to be unraveled, in which case we are subjected to endless discussions, our lives examined by researchers zealous for the clue that will account for our lack of health or happiness.

The gospel offers a different view of suffering: in suffering we enter *the depths;* we are at the heart of things; we are near to where Christ was on the cross.

And so we find in Psalm 130 not so much as a trace of those things that are so common among us, which rob us of our humanity when we suffer and make the pain so much more terrible to bear. No glib smart answers. No lectures on our misfortunes in which we are hauled into a classroom and given graduate courses in suffering. No hasty Band-Aid treatments covering up our trouble so that the rest of society does not have to look at it. Neither prophets nor priests nor psalmists offer quick cures for the suffering: we don't find any of them telling us to take a vacation, use this drug, get a hobby. Nor do they ever engage in publicity cover-ups, the plastic-smile propaganda campaigns that hide trouble behind a billboard of positive thinking. None of that: the suffering is held up and proclaimed—and prayed.

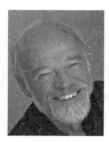 **Eugene H. Peterson** (1932–2018) was a pastor, scholar, author, and poet. He wrote more than thirty books, including his widely acclaimed paraphrase of the Bible, *The Message*; his memoir, *The Pastor*; and numerous works of biblical spiritual formation, including *Run with the Horses*.

IMAGING GOD

TARA BETH LEACH, *RADIANT CHURCH*

*So if I, your Lord and Teacher, have washed your
feet, you also ought to wash one another's feet.*

JOHN 13:14

Many have wrestled with some portraits of God found in Scripture—that is, those portraits of a violent and vengeful God. These images can be profoundly oppressive for a Christian. But when we look to the cross, things begin to change.

The cross—an upside-down display of power and "foolishness to those who are perishing" (1 Corinthians 1:18 NIV)—reveals the very nature and heart of God.

Our pictures of God matter. They shape our witness. If the people of God are to be *imitators* of God, then our images of God matter all the more. As we read through the Gospels, we discover that every Gospel account is headed to the cross. It's not just building in the event itself but in the teachings, miracles, and actions of Jesus. So, by the time they arrive at the cross, the disciples begin to grapple with the teachings they had been wrestling with all along. Jesus' disciples now recognize the way of the cross all the way to the bitter end. As we build toward the cross, and as Jesus reveals the way of the cross through his teachings and actions, he pushes the disciples to go and do likewise. This is perhaps most highlighted in the "Way of the Cross Teachings" in the Gospel of Mark (see Mark 8–10). Jesus reveals that he must suffer; so must they. Jesus must lay down his life; so must they. Jesus must carry his cross; so must they.

We also see this type of modeling and commanding in John 13. On the same night Jesus would be betrayed, he gathered around the table with the disciples.

Jesus is modeling that the way of the cross isn't an abstract idea, but it's to be lived in community, usually counterculturally, and often uncomfortably. But Jesus calls his people to live this way, and it's the way he modeled.

When our vision of Jesus is in line with the Scripture's vision, it alters and disrupts our lives. Like Paul's encounter on the road to Damascus, the scales on our eyes begin to fall away, and we learn to see that the way of Jesus is the way of the cross and often is drastically different from our distorted images of God. It matters who we are imitating.

When we truly behold the radiant image of Jesus, we are transformed into his radiant image. Behold, dear church. Let us behold the one and true image of God—Jesus. Let us fall in love with the Jesus of Scripture. Let us be a people who saturate in the Gospels, memorize the teachings of Jesus, and align ourselves with the way of the cross.

Tara Beth Leach is a pastor at Christ Church of Oak Brook and previously served as senior pastor of First Church of the Nazarene of Pasadena. Leach is author of *Emboldened* and *Forty Days on Being a Six*, and is a regular writer for Missio Alliance.

....

FULLY ALIVE

JUANITA CAMPBELL RASMUS, *LEARNING TO BE*

In him we live and move and have our being.

ACTS 17:28 NIV

I had been running on empty for a long time. Not until I hit rock bottom did I realize that the gas gauge within me was damaged. I needed a deeper reality. I was beginning to know the meaning of Acts 17:28.

My being is the me that manifested in divine love at my conception. In Christ there is fullness of life, not the coma that I had lived through rote activity and damning rules. I had lived as though my activities sourced my life—as though they gave me life—only to find that while they may have seemed like *good* activities, in time they literally drained the life out of me. I needed to be recharged, but I didn't know this until I was on empty; hitting the bottom helped me to know what my empty was like.

Some folks have a longer battery life than others. Perhaps their lives are not so demanding. Perhaps some of us are poorly charged for the tasks of life awaiting us. Or we start out of the gate at such a pace that by our midthirties we find ourselves depleted. For all my life to this point I had presumed that *my* effort sustained me, crazy as it sounds. But through the depression, I was being freed from those notions of self-sustainability. Thank God for this awakening. In the depth of the darkness I found my being in the presence of God. I knew intuitively that all I was had been in God alone. It was clear that in the same way the lotus flower blooms in muddy waters, God brought me to life amid the muddiness of my rules, perfectionism, and striving. There was nothing in that awareness but pure gratitude, relief really. Now I knew where my sustenance was coming from, and I was being fueled and filled.

I had been parched by life, sucked dry. I was humbled, grateful beyond words, thrilled speechless in the presence of God who was quenching in me a thirst that only God could satisfy. I was being energized and charged to live and move and to know what it meant to be fully alive. God met me at the level of my thirst. There was no effort on my part, no scheduling, no doing, no talking, just being, and being fully aware that that was all I needed. My aliveness was God's doing, and being was my response.

God was instructing me to stop *doing* and just *be*.

 **Juanita Campbell Rasmus** copastors St. John's United Methodist Church with her husband, Rudy. She is also the author of *Forty Days on Being a One*. Juanita has served as a member of the board of directors of Renovaré, the board of Houston Graduate School of Theology, and advisory boards for Rice University's Religion and Public Life Program and re:MIND Houston.

RIGHTEOUS RISK

CHRISTINA BARLAND EDMONDSON AND
CHAD BRENNAN, *FAITHFUL ANTIRACISM*

These I will bring to my holy mountain
and give them joy in my house of prayer.

ISAIAH 56:7 NIV

Jesus' stand for justice was not limited, partial, or inconsistent. In chapters 20–22 of Matthew, we learn about Jesus' final journey to Jerusalem for his death and resurrection. While in Jerusalem, Jesus cleansed the temple of merchants who had turned it into a "den of robbers" (Matthew 21:13 NIV). Jesus, the fulfillment of the Law and the Prophets, pointed back to Isaiah 56:7. Additionally, the phrase "den of robbers" comes from Jeremiah 7:11, where God is rebuking the people, specifically the temple leaders, for their abuses and oppression of the needy. Combining these two reference points sheds light on an additional dimension of Jesus' words at the temple. His rebuke is specifically addressing the oppression of the poor and foreigners within the temple. This background helps us to understand the true catalyst of Christ's anger that led to him flipping the tables.

While in Jerusalem, Jesus also rebuked the religious leadership (scribes and Pharisees) for their hypocrisy, pride, hunger for recognition, misguided evangelistic zeal, superficial religiosity, greed, self-indulgence, and neglect of justice. His rebuke included:

> Woe to you, teachers of the law and Pharisees, you hypocrites! You give a tenth of your spices—mint, dill and cumin. But you have neglected the more important matters of the law—justice, mercy and faithfulness. You should have practiced the latter, without neglecting the former.... You clean the outside of the cup and dish, but inside they are full of greed and self-indulgence. (Matthew 23:23–25 NIV)

Of course, Jesus took an enormous risk by pointing out the ways that the powerful religious leaders in his day were leading people away from God's will. In fact, soon after he made those comments, the religious leaders played a central role in having him arrested and crucified. But that did not stop Jesus from taking a stand for what he knew was correct.

Christina Barland Edmondson is a higher education instructor and organizational consultant on ethics, equity, and Christian leadership development. She holds a PhD in counseling psychology and is cohost of the *Truth's Table* podcast.

Chad Brennan is coordinator of the Race, Religion, and Justice Project, and founder of Renew Partnerships, focusing on diversity in faith-based organizations.

BREATH PRAYER

BREATHE IN

Your will and kingdom.

BREATHE OUT

On earth as in heaven.

A GREAT CLOUD OF TRUTH TELLERS

[1]We are surrounded by a great cloud of truth tellers *who have shown us what it means to trust the Great Spirit.* So let us lay to the side everything that weighs us down and the broken ways that so easily wrap around *our legs to trip us.* And let us run as if we are in a long-distance race, setting a steady pace and heading toward the goal.

[2]This means we must keep our eyes on Creator Sets Free (Jesus), the trailblazer of our spiritual ways,[a] the one who was first to reach the end of the trail. The joy that lay before him gave him the strength to suffer on the cross and willingly bear its shame. He now sits at Creator's right hand in the place of greatest honor.

[3]If you will keep your thoughts on how much hostility Creator Sets Free (Jesus) endured from those with bad hearts and broken ways, it will keep you from growing weary and your hearts from falling to the ground.

HEBREWS 12:1-3 FNV

BEING THE BROKEN BODY

SOONG-CHAN RAH, *PROPHETIC LAMENT*

While they were eating, he took a loaf of bread, and after blessing it he broke it, gave it to them, and said, "Take; this is my body." Then he took a cup, and after giving thanks he gave it to them, and all of them drank from it. He said to them, "This is my blood of the covenant, which is poured out for many."

MARK 14:22-24

The church has the power to bring healing in a racially fragmented society. That power is not found in an emphasis on strength but in suffering and weakness. The difficult topic of racial reconciliation requires the intersection of celebration and suffering. The Lord's Table provides the opportunity for the church to operate at the intersection of celebration and suffering. In 1 Corinthians 11:26, we are reminded that we have the opportunity to "proclaim the Lord's death." In remembering Jesus' suffering on our behalf, we discover our mutual and common dependence on the body of Christ broken for us. It is not merely the symbolic act of the Lord's Table that unites us, but the commitment to that broken body and the actual embodiment of unity. The suffering narrative that informs the

Lord's Table is an expression of lament that is necessary for the unity found in the body of Christ, but the necessary condition for the celebration of the Lord's Supper is lament.

Lamentations recognizes that hope can arise in the midst of suffering because of God's faithfulness. Celebration can arise out of suffering, but lament is a necessary expression of that suffering. In a triumphalistic world, Lamentations makes no sense. The theology of celebration will always be more attractive than the theology of suffering. But if lament were offered to a suffering world, the hope that is woven into lament offers the possibility of genuine reconciliation.

Soong-Chan Rah is the Robert Boyd Munger Professor of Evangelism at Fuller Theological Seminary. He has served on the boards of World Vision, Sojourners, the Christian Community Development Association, and the Catalyst Leadership Center. He is also author of *The Next Evangelicalism* and *Many Colors*.

FELLOW SUFFERING

MUNTHER ISAAC, *THE OTHER SIDE OF THE WALL*

*From noon on, darkness came over the whole land until
three in the afternoon. And about three o'clock Jesus
cried with a loud voice, "Eli, Eli, lema sabachthani?" that
is, "My God, my God, why have you forsaken me?"*

MATTHEW 27:45-46

We live in a day and age full of religious extremism, where
many suffer at the hands of religion and power. During
the Easter season in Palestine, I always remind my congregants
that Jesus himself died as a victim of religious violence and
intolerance. We often forget this, that the crime Jesus was con-
victed of was blasphemy. I also remind them that the religious
institution needed the political institution—the Herods of our
world today—to achieve its purpose. It was the unholy marriage between religion and politics that ultimately killed Jesus.

The cross shows us that Jesus suffers with us. He is no stranger
to religious extremism, nor to political tyrants. Just like he
walked with Daniel's three friends in the furnace of fire, today
he walks with us in our hardships. He suffers with us and gives
us strength. And when Jesus was on the cross, he embraced his

death, for he knew that this death would bring us life. On the cross, Jesus also experienced the silence of God. He cried, "My Lord, my Lord, why have you forsaken me?" Is it not the same question that the land of Palestine has been crying out over the years—"God, where are you?"—that Jesus asked when he was on the cross? "Where are you God?"

The cross reminds us that God is in solidarity with the oppressed, with the victims of religious violence and state violence. In Jesus, God walked in solidarity and suffered with those rejected and pushed to the other side. And in the cross, we remember that we are not alone. God walks with us in our own "valley of the shadow of death."

As we walk in the valley of the shadow of death till the end of our road today, we pray and beg to experience Jesus placing his hand upon our free shoulders.

Munther Isaac is the academic dean of Bethlehem Bible College in Palestine. He is also pastor of Christmas Evangelical Lutheran Church and author of *From Land to Lands, from Eden to the Renewed Earth.*

THE QUIET BEFORE
THE OUTCOME

ESAU McCAULLEY, *LENT*

Do you work wonders for the dead?
Do the shades rise up to praise you?

PSALM 88:10

In times of trauma, aren't we tempted to wonder if this particular problem is too big for God? God may have been sufficient when we were younger, but what can he do when our marriage is in trouble or the loneliness of another year stretches before us? What will God do about the darkness in our heart that we just can't shake? When will he do something about the pain we see all around?

The disciples must have considered these questions on Holy Saturday. They hid for a reason. They "had hoped that he was the one who was going to redeem Israel" (Luke 24:21), but now all appeared lost. The crucifixion of Jesus seemed to be a tragedy so all-encompassing there was no future. What good were all those things he had taught them if death still ruled over him? The experience of the disciples in the wake of Jesus' death stands in for all our disappointments. We too have moments when it appears as if God failed us. There are seemingly unanswered prayers that will trouble us until we see him face-to-face.

The good news of Holy Saturday is not that the disciples waited with faith. They did not. Often, we do not either. There are moments when the traumas in our lives are too much and we are overcome with despair. Sometimes it is all just too much for us.

But God does not share our anxieties. The latest theory claiming to disprove his existence does not trouble him nor do supposed threats to his power. As the psalm reminds us, "He who sits in the heavens laughs; the Lord has them in derision" (Psalm 2:4 NRSV). Christ knew he would rise again. If the experience of the disciples stands in for our fears, then the peace of Christ serves as God's answer to our troubled hearts. We can be at peace because God reigns even over the death that unnerves us. We end Lent with the confidence that all will be well.

This is how the season of Lent concludes. Things are quiet. We are silent. We stand at the tomb wondering what God will do next. Whether we have kept our fasts or failed has no bearing on the final outcome. God either has the power to raise Christ from the dead, or he does not. We are Christians because we have concluded that he does. That means we can rest.

Esau McCaulley is associate professor of New Testament at Wheaton College and a contributing opinion writer for the *New York Times*. He is also the editor of the Fullness of Time book series on the church year and the author of *Lent*, the first volume in that series.

RECOGNITION

SHARON GARLOUGH BROWN, *REMEMBER ME*

*Jesus said to her, "Mary!" She turned and said to him
in Hebrew, "Rabbouni!" (which means Teacher).*

JOHN 20:16

Resurrection never comes as we expect. I think of Mary
Magdalene weeping at the tomb, new grief layered upon
fresh sorrow. Jesus isn't where they left him! Now what? Then,
even when she sees him and is overcome with joy and relief, he
tells her not to cling to him. If I had been Mary, I don't think I
would have obeyed. If I thought I'd lost him once, only to get
him back, I don't think I would have easily let him go again.
And yet, letting go always sits at the core of our journeys,
painful as it is.

I've been thinking today, too, about how grief and bewil-
derment can veil our sight and keep us from noticing the ways
Jesus does appear with resurrection life. For Mary, she didn't
recognize him until he spoke her name. The disciples on the
road to Emmaus didn't recognize him until he took the bread
and broke it for them. Thomas needed to see his wounds. And
I've needed the gift of community to help me see his presence

in the midst of desolation. Even then, it's often only in retrospect that I glimpse how he has kept me company, as he did—incognito—with the heartbroken, disappointed disciples trudging their way to Emmaus from Jerusalem. He gently asks questions, refuses to rush me to joy, and opens the Word to reveal the mystery of God's providence. Often, only in retrospect do I see how my own heart burned with recognition, even when my mind did not—or could not—perceive him.

And so, dear one, we keep watch in all the gardens where we've planted our sorrow, and we wait to see what he will do. What a gift to keep watch and wait in hope together.

Sharon Garlough Brown is a spiritual director, speaker, and cofounder of Abiding Way Ministries. She is the author of the bestselling Sensible Shoes series. Sharon has served on the pastoral staff of congregations in Scotland, Oklahoma, England, and in West Michigan, where she copastored with her husband, Jack.

SOURCES

Excerpts from InterVarsity Press books are as follows:

Introduction: Quotations from Adele Ahlberg Calhoun. *Spiritual Disciplines Handbook.* Revised and expanded edition. ©2015 by Adele Ahlberg Calhoun; and Esau McCaulley. *Lent.* ©2023 by Esau D. McCaulley.

Ash Wednesday: Tish Harrison Warren. *Prayer in the Night.* ©2021 by Tish Harrison Warren.

Thursday: Esau McCaulley. *Reading While Black.* ©2020 by Esau D. McCaulley.

Friday: Sheila Wise Rowe. *Young, Gifted, and Black.* ©2021 by Sheila Wise Rowe.

Saturday: Ruth Haley Barton. *Embracing Rhythms of Work and Rest.* ©2022 by Ruth Haley Barton.

WEEK ONE

Monday: Dominique DuBois Gilliard. *Rethinking Incarceration.* ©2018 by Dominique Gilliard.

Thursday: Marlena Graves. *The Way Up Is Down.* ©2020 by Marlena Graves.

Friday: John M. Perkins. *Welcoming Justice.* ©2009 by Charles Marsh and John M. Perkins.

Saturday: Drew Jackson. *God Speaks Through Wombs.* ©2021 by Drew Edward Jackson.

WEEK TWO

Monday: Joshua Choonmin Kang. *Deep-Rooted in Christ.* ©2007 by Joshua Choonmin Kang.

Wednesday: Donna Barber. *Bread for the Resistance.* ©2019 by Donna Marie Barber.

Friday: Natasha Sistrunk Robinson. *A Sojourner's Truth.* ©2018 by Natasha Sistrunk Robinson.

Saturday: Dan Stringer. *Struggling with Evangelicalism.* ©2021 by Daniel Stringer.

WEEK THREE

Monday: Tish Harrison Warren. *Liturgy of the Ordinary.* ©2016 by Tish Harrison Warren.

Thursday: Graham Hill and Grace Ji-Sun Kim. *Healing Our Broken Humanity.* ©2018 by Graham J. G. Hill and Grace Ji-Sun Kim.

Friday: Mark E. Strong. *Divine Merger.* ©2016 by Mark E. Strong.

Saturday: Sheila Wise Rowe. *Healing Racial Trauma.* ©2019 by Sheila Wise Rowe.

WEEK FOUR

Monday: Bethany H. Hoang. *Deepening the Soul for Justice.* ©2012 by International Justice Mission.

Thursday: Gregory Coles. *No Longer Strangers.* ©2021 by Gregory Coles.

Friday: Brenda Salter McNeil. *A Credible Witness.* ©2008 by Brenda Salter McNeil.

Saturday: Sandra Maria Van Opstal. *The Next Worship.* ©2015 by Sandra Maria Van Opstal.

WEEK FIVE

Monday: Ruth Haley Barton. *Life Together in Christ.* ©2014 by Ruth Haley Barton.

Thursday: Eugene H. Peterson. *A Long Obedience in the Same Direction.* Second edition. ©2000 by Eugene H. Peterson.

Friday: Tara Beth Leach. *Radiant Church.* ©2021 by Tara Beth Leach.

Saturday: Juanita Campbell Rasmus. *Learning to Be.* ©2020 by Juanita Campbell Rasmus.

WEEK SIX

Monday: Chad Brennan and Christina Edmondson. *Faithful Antiracism.* ©2022 by Chad Brennan and Christina Edmondson.

Maundy Thursday: Soong-Chan Rah. *Prophetic Lament.* ©2015 by Soong-Chan Rah.

Good Friday: Munther Isaac. *The Other Side of the Wall.* ©2020 by Munther Isaac.

Holy Saturday: Esau McCaulley. *Lent.* ©2023 by Esau D. McCaulley.

Easter Sunday: Sharon Garlough Brown. *Remember Me.* ©2019 by Sharon Garlough Brown.